WHAT PEOPLE ARE SAYING ABOUT THE BOOK BLOW YOUR OWN HORN

"When it comes to speaking in pub' ... ıg about the topic and fewer still have t ... y and grace of the man. I applaud him ... e writes and listening to every word he

— Jay Conra

"In my experience as a marketing cons... ..., speaking is the #1 best source of new clients and hot sales leads for most people. The next best quality source is a published book which people pay money for. Internet leads and other advertising sources fall below those two. So if you're looking for an immediate business boost, mastering speaking is one of the best things you can do. Very early in the book, Michael says, "Did you ever see Barack Obama, Churchill, Nelson Mandela or Tony Blair ever use slides?" Duh. Now I realize why I've never liked Power Point. He goes on to enunciate specific guidelines for modulating voice, pace and content. Michael's tips on notes are very useful, and not perhaps what you'd expect: He recommends pictures and flow charts over words, so that you can engage your audience with 95% eye contact.

This is not a motivational book that extolls the virtues of becoming a skilled speaker; it's a short, digestible hands-on manual. Anyone nervous about speaking won't be after reading this book."

— Perry Marshall
Author of The Ultimate Guide to Google Adwords
and the world's most-quoted consultant on Google Advertising.

"I am fortunate in that I have worked at companies that employed Michael Trigg to improve the presentation skills of senior management. He did an excellent job then. For those who are not fortunate enough to have him teaching them in person, this book is an excellent way to improve confidence in presentational skills. A helpful,powerful book but one which is very easy to read."

— David Somers, Non Executive Director, Europe Arab Bank
and Trustee of Fujitsu Technologies Pension Fund,

"Having to present can fill me with dread, but the techniques in this book get me through time and time again until I can start to believe I'm actually good at it. I've been lucky enough to have been trained by Michael and use his book to remind myself of all the best-practices he teaches. The book's great, quick and easy to read and to flick to chapters when you're looking at working on a specific bit of a presentation. Having used the techniques - and seen those that don't - I know that this book will put anyone head and shoulders above other presenters."

— Chris Gibbs, Senior Account Director, Waggener Edstrom

"Presenting is something that is feared! Take the advice given here and fear no more. It is not very often that you come across a book that delivers so succinctly on its core objective; so much so that you can open on any page and a little gem of an idea or action comes out. A gem of a book, for anyone wanting to communicate better, at any level."

— John Greenshaw, MD, Merlin Telecommunications

"A super book, practical advice to implement immediately. Michael Trigg give you what you need to become a true professional. Quite simply, excellent. If you are looking for a practical, clear and concise guide to presenting - one that will not only greatly improve the quality of your presentations but also significantly reduce the time you take preparing - then Blow Your Own Horn is the book to buy. I challenge anyone who reads this book not to notice an immediate improvement in their ability to deliver effective presentations."

— Luke Thomson, Director, Head of Markit Economics

SUNMAKERS

THE 13 KEY SECRETS OF POWERFUL PRESENTING

MICHAEL TRIGG

SUNMAKERS

THE 13 SECRETS OF POWERFUL PRESENTING

Published by Sunmakers, a division of Eldamar Ltd,
157 Oxford Road, Cowley, Oxford, OX4 2ES, UK
www.sunmakers.co.uk
Tel +44(0)1865 779944

First Edition

Designed by Ayd Instone, www.sunmakers.co.uk

ISBN: 978-1-908693-13-6

www.presentationskillscoaching.co.uk

To all who just want to get their message out there

– and to stand out from the crowd.

"When it comes to speaking in public, few people know as much as Michael Trigg about the topic and fewer still have the ability to put it into words with the accuracy and grace of the man. I applaud him and highly recommend reading every word he writes and listening to every word he says."

— Jay Conrad Levinson, The Father of Guerilla Marketing

Contents

GIVING YOU THE PRESENTATION ADVANTAGE

We really do live in an unfair world. The best qualified person or team and the best product or service should always win the day. Sometimes they do, yet frequently they don't. And much of why they don't is down to the lacklustre, confused and colourless way that they present and pitch.

It is the WAY something is presented that creates a winning edge.

You might think that you are about to read a treatise on the dark arts, containing all manner of devious techniques. Well, I'm sorry to disappoint you!

However, what you now have in your hands or on your screen are highly pragmatic, powerful, tried and tested tools for giving you that edge.

In these 13 Key Secrets I have distilled the essence of what it takes to give yourself an advantage over your internal and external competition - the Presentation Advantage.

You'll notice how very few people use even a handful of them.

So put them to work for you this week and experience how EASY they are to apply and the difference they make.

SECRET NO.1

DIFFERENTIATE YOURSELF

Businesses ultimately fail or succeed through sales - clients wanting to buy and use their services and products or ideas. Being able to win and retain clients is crucial. Far too often, almost total reliance is placed on "The Three Ps" - process, procedure and Powerpoint - these neither touch the soul nor ignite the imagination. Are you guilty of relying on them?

Benjamin Franklin said "If you seek to persuade, appeal to the interest rather than the intellect." We teach you how to influence with integrity, whilst building a relationship. So often what we have to sell or offer is very similar if not identical to what our competition offers. The fees are similar, the product similar, the client list, the track record, the sort of people working for the organisation....so why should the client choose you?

Many reasons, but rarely are they to do with fees, process or the product. It often has much much more to do with how you engage - how well they feel understood - how you talk plain English - how safe they feel to ask questions - how well you package the message so that they understand where you are coming from and where you want to go. These sort of things create the difference that makes the difference.

Let me give you a real example. One of my clients - a major branding agency - had a potential client say .. "Listen, I know you can do the work. And I know the four other agencies I'll be interviewing can do the work too. What I'm looking to decide is "Do I want to work with you for the next three years?"

What do you think your client might say?

Would he choose you rather than your competition?

SECRET NO.2

BE UNDERSTOOD AND REMEMBERED POSITIVELY - TALK A LANGUAGE EVERYONE CAN UNDERSTAND

Do you ever find yourself on the receiving end of a presentation about a subject you know well - and wonder what on earth they are talking about? Or maybe you do this to your own hapless audiences!

It is SO easy to fall into the unhelpful trap of speaking jargon – technospeak, banking speak, legalese. Every sector and every organisation often delights in creating its own unique collection of three letter abbreviations and a language and phraseology of its own. These are not only baffling and irritating to clients and outsiders, they frequently baffle, confuse and mislead partners, team members and colleagues.

Example : I worked with one of the star fund managers of a major investment bank. He was technically brilliant at what he did, but reticent and shy in promoting his ideas, as well as using far too much investment and banking jargon. After just 3 coaching sessions together, he made a major presentation to fellow fund managers, directors and any bank personnel who wished to attend. The marketing director of this bank, an

American lady, was part of the audience and was observed saying afterwards" That's the first ******* presentation I've understood in this bank for two years!"

A good rule of thumb is to imagine that your audience is about 17 years old, extremely intelligent and with a very low boredom threshold and doesn't know a great deal about what you do. If you can hold the attention of an audience of 17 year olds for the length of your presentation, then you're doing well.

SECRET NO.3

HAVE A STRONG START

I've often heard it said that one should "start the talk with a Bang." That can work, it depends on the context. The danger is that the "Bang" turns out to be a whimper and misses the target by miles.

In most cases, your introduction needs some form of statement which hooks audience interest and attention, leading into the topic that you intend to talk about. It doesn't have to be long - or witty - but it does need to be ear catching and at least a little intriguing.

For example: "We've been making it for centuries. The prices it commands can be astronomical. Volumes have been written about its beauty and complexity. And it all begins with one simple little berry, the grape. And in particular, the Cabernet Sauvignon - and it's this grape, and what it can produce - that is the subject of this presentation."

Then introduce yourself if need be. Many start off with their name as the first words they utter. That's not wrong, but it isn't going to grab audience attention. Better to hook their attention first as shown above, THEN you can introduce yourself.

The next piece in the sequence is probably the most important - tell your audience the purpose or the aim of the presentation ie: what they can gain from listening to you, what you expect them to do or think differently as a result of giving you their time. Finally, lay out your agenda - what you'll be covering. With precious few exceptions, keep it to 3 agenda items. Why so few? They won't remember any more than 3.

All of this will probably take between 30-90 seconds - no longer. Much shorter and you won't do your introduction justice. Too long, and people are wondering where you are and when you're going to start!

If you would like to purchase all 13 Secrets in a Kindle format, please jump over to Amazon today.

SECRET NO.4

HAVE A MESSAGE

Think back to the last ten presentations you sat through. How many of them were crystal clear in their message? Do YOUR talks have one every time? If you asked someone to stand at the door and quiz the people on their way out - what message would they be taking away?

Ask some of your colleagues why they are giving a presentation and just listen to the answers. "It's the monthly meeting", "It's part of my job", "It's the first Tuesday of the month", "Because my boss asked me to", "Because my team expect it". In other words, they don't have one!

Every talk needs an AIM - a message. There is only one AIM and it needs to be crystal clear. A good way to phrase it might be "What I'd like to achieve over the next 20 mins is to X so that you are better able to Y."

SECRET NO.5

MAKING MORE OF "YOU" AVAILABLE

There is something inside all of us which engages more willingly with a speaker when they are being themselves, rather than putting on an act. Of course, we can be enthralled and moved by great and even good acting. That is why we pay to go to the theatre - it's entrancing. But we know the context - and we know they are acting - and we are paying them to "act." A presentation is not acting, it's about being natural .Yes, we will talk louder to a room full of people than we would across a dinner table, but it should still be natural.

How to do this? There are many facets, but the most powerful tools to allow the real you to come across are:

• a fool proof structure and message

• a note format that allows you to say all that you want, without being tied to a script or slides as described in the book Blow Your Own Horn - available on Amazon as a paperback and Kindle.

The method that I teach literally programmes your brain with the content, and it comes out in the right sequence and without you having to refer to the notes. The content is already there in your brain - and your brain just delivers, as if by magic. Once you have experienced the sheer power and simplicity of this technique, and it only takes a couple of times for you to know it works, then more of you becomes naturally available to the audience. Your audience will love it.

SECRET NO.6

PAUSE

Most of us are at least a little apprehensive when presenting, and some of us are petrified. And one of the side effects of adrenalin pumping round our system is the effect it has on our perception of time. It distorts it.

When we are nervous, what appears to be a perfectly decent pause to you, the speaker, is unnoticeable to the audience.

Why does this matter?

Simple. We want to engage our audience. We want to achieve our aim, we want them to get the "what's in it for them". We want to be not only heard, but understood and remembered. Now here's the thing. There is only so much any brain can absorb at any one time - however intelligent and brilliant. And we need to receive our information in chunks. Bite sized mouthfuls. We need mental space to think, to consider, to muse, to compare with what we know already, to say to ourselves "Hmmm, that's true/interesting etc" before being ready to receive the next mental mouthful.

If you do not pause enough, you will cause your audience to get frustrated and even angry, because you are not giving them the mental space to digest what you are telling them.

Imagine a bowl of muesli in front of you for breakfast. You and I both know that such a dish requires a lot of milk to lubricate it and a great deal of chewing through all the nuts and seeds and grain before it's ready to swallow.

How would you respond to someone really bossy who said you had only 90 seconds to eat that whole bowl, and that you are only allowed an egg cup full of milk to wash it down? Not an enticing prospect. But this is what you do to people's brains when you don't pause for long enough. So.....PAUSE for longer than feels comfortable.

SECRET NO.7

SIGNPOSTING

So simple, so powerful - yet rarely practised.

You can start brilliantly, have your audience keen and engaged, yet lose them all too easily if they cannot follow where they are in your talk. Avoid all attempts to be subtle here. Imagine them looking like two old fashioned street signs on a pole - pointing at 180 degrees from each other - one up the street and one down. In practise it would sound like this....

"Now that was some tips about Pauses......now let me move onto point 7, which is all about the importance of Signposting.....PAUSE......."

If you are too swift or subtle, your audience will not have noticed the change in direction/topic and will easily become confused as to where they or you are. And a confused audience is not going to be a happy one - unless you're telling lots of jokes and they don't care!

SECRET NO.8

KEEP YOUR ENERGY HIGH

Easily said and easily done. There are many breathing and visualisation exercises you can do, some excellent and some useless. I am not going to address these, I'm going to suggest something simpler, easier and just as powerful. And it's this.

Keep your volume high. If you speak loudly enough, it has several highly useful effects. Firstly, it is the major part of the authority in your voice. It is nigh on impossible to sound knowledgeable and enthusiastic if you talk softly - unless you have massive position power, like Don Corleone, or Stalin. But the chances are that you don't possess huge position power. Even if you did, it would be rash and arrogant to rely just on this to provide the power and gravitas for your talk.

Secondly, when you speak louder you are better able to engage all of the room. I know it sounds obvious, but it is too easy to assume that you are talking loud enough. Everything is context dependent - culture, size of room, size of audience, acoustics, background noise.

But here are a couple of secrets. Be aware of the soft or hard nature of the environment or room where you are presenting.

Most corporate environments are "hard" - there is often plenty of glass and wood, which reflect sound easily, the carpets are rarely plush and do not absorb sound easily. It is the "soft" environments that can easily muffle a speaker - soft, comfy furniture, thick plush curtains. These soak up the sound like a sponge - as do the audience. People too are like sponges for sound, so the larger the audience (20 and above) the more you will need to talk louder and louder still.

3 months ago I was invited to rehearse and coach a new CEO for a crucial talk to 150 of his staff, and we had never met before. He could only give me 90 minutes the evening before he was to give one of the most important talks of his life. This man was taking over the top position of a company with many problems, shaky morale, fears of job security and more. Not only did he need to address these issues but also make his mark and establish his credibility as the new CEO.

We did the rehearsal in the large empty conference room which could seat about 300. The audience chairs were arranged in four to five rows, slightly semicircle and from memory about 35-40 chairs. He stood on the podium and started to talk, and even with no one else apart from the two of us in the room, I could not hear him. I asked him to start again and double the volume. Still not much better. I asked him to double it again. And again. And again. Four times.

Only then was he just loud enough to reach the back of the room and to convey the authority and enthusiasm he needed. He just couldn't believe it. But he did what was needed. I called him the next day to ask how things went. Not only did it go very well, he had 15-20 people come up to him and shake his hand and thank him for his honesty, clarity and the human touch. He also received some 25 emails saying similar things. I think you'll agree that sort of response is pretty rare - and we'd only spent about 90 minutes together. I since went on to work with him and his confidence, gravitas and professionalism have increased three fold.

I have done the same thing countless times with clients. It's a very common misconception that just to raise the loudness of your voice by 50% is enough for a bigger room. It isn't. Every environment will have it's own volume requirement - make sure you judge your volume accordingly.

When your volume is high enough, it ensures that your energy is high too - they go together. And an energetic talk is infinitely more engaging than a low energy one.

If you would like a copy of all 13 Secrets, you can get hold of your own copy on Kindle, over on Amazon. Click here to go there now.

SECRET NO.9

VARY YOUR INTONATION

Absolutely crucial. The importance of this varies from culture to culture. Welsh and Italians tend to have a musical lilt to their voice and very varied intonation and pitch. The Finns, Bulgarians and some English less so.

Your pitch or intonation is the "music" in your voice - the interest factor. Vary it slightly more than you would in every day speech. Imagine you are telling a joke to your friends in a bar, or engaging with interest across a lunch table - would you have a flat, boring pitch?

Of course not. So avoid doing that in a presentation. One of the best and easiest ways to ensure that your pitch varies is to keep your volume higher than normal - have you ever tried talking loud with a flat pitch to your voice? Go on - try it. It's almost impossible!

So vary your pitch and keep your volume high - both will help you to engage and enthuse your audience.

Don't forget the Kindle version of my 13 Secrets available on Amazon today. Click here for more information.

SECRET NO.10

BE ENGAGED AND ENGAGING

Any presenter has 3 major obligations or duties to their audience. One of them is to be natural, to be you, not to act. Another is to get your message across. The third is to be interesting and engaging.

We've addressed the first two, now let's deal with the third. So how do you become interesting?

Well, be interested in the subject and let that show. But there are times when we have to deliver stuff that definitely isn't too interesting - often around policies and procedures - although for some, these can be fascinating. Whatever floats your boat! If you find yourself in the position of talking about stuff that bores you, then be aware - it leaks. It shows. And if YOU aren't engaged by it, how can you expect your audience to be?

So, when faced with this from time to time - as most of us are - then be BRIEF. Get through it quickly, so there is less chance of your lack of interest leaking out. Much better to do that than bore everyone and yourself by wading through turgid material. It's hard to get them back once you lose them. So avoid losing them in the first place.

How do you engage? Come across with some energy (volume) and enthusiasm. Avoid being false, but do ramp up the energy and say what YOU want to say - rather than a presentation that someone else has "written" for you. It is very hard to enthuse sincerely from another's material. That doesn't mean that you have to reinvent the wheel, but do use your own "voice" and style. Resist wherever possible the edicts of others to put you into a stylistic straight jacket. Of course, your company wants you to stay "on message" - but that doesn't mean that you need sound like a talking glove puppet - which many do. You know this - you've heard them! If you're unlucky, you may even work for or with them.

Come across with genuine sparkle and enthusiasm - and your own unique style. You won't have to work at this - it is natural.

That's the secret. And to allow yourself to be natural and willing to engage, its good to be engaged in your subject. Know your content well, but not word perfect - you need some spontaneity. Have a good start and powerful structure that works for you and supports you. You'll find this explained in the booklet *Stand Out from the Crowd - 99 Tips for Effective and Powerful Presenting* - available on Kindle, Amazon and iTunes.

In summary, vary your pitch and pace, vary your volume and PAUSE.

1
A2
A3
O
X

SECRET NO.11

LOOK AT EVERYONE

This is one the most powerful Secrets of all. It is so obvious, yet few do this well.

What are the typical traps?

One of the biggest mistakes is to look too much at your screen or slides. Far too many people use the slides as their notes. In fact the way they prepare is to create a host of slides, then wonder how to talk round them.

Wrong.

Get your ideas, the start, the message/aim and content headings together first on paper. Decide what these are and THEN make your notes. LAST of all, create your slides.

Other pitfalls include finding a friendly face and dwelling too long on them, failing to look at those on either side of you, being buried in or worse reading your notes. When presenting sitting across a table or to a small group, there is often a strong temptation just to focus on the senior person there.

Wrong.

By all means give them good eye contact, but ALWAYS look at every one else round the table as well. If they are part of the audience, then they are almost sure to be part of the decision making.

You are most unlikely to know the true dynamics across the table. If you avoid looking at someone, they are going to feel unengaged, ignored or both. When you leave the room and they talk and decide, if you haven't looked at them, they are going to make negative comments and judgements - and lessen the chance of you securing or keeping the business.

SECRET NO.12

USE PICTORIAL, COLOURFUL NOTES, NOT SOLELY THE WRITTEN WORD

Highly effective notes are one of the most useful and powerful tools to build confidence, fluency and effectiveness.

In general, the notes that most people use for presenting are not even worth the paper they are written on.

A strong statement but 28 years of experience has shown me this. Mostly they are too wordy, one colour (monotone) and just not fit for purpose - unless you are going to read them like a speech. Reading a speech is an art in itself, and as you can see from television, most have not mastered it. I do not teach the reading of speeches and talks, but if that is what you need - and how to use autocues - then I am happy to recommend those who specialise in it.

What I teach is how to create foolproof notes that allow you to cover everything, miss nothing, engage the audience with eye contact 95% of the time, never lose your way or be stuck for words, be fluent, natural and enthusiastic - and look as if you are being spontaneous and making it up as you go. Oh, and this method cuts your preparation time by up to 90%. It is almost magical and works every time.

But for now, allow yourself to make your notes colourful and pictorial - using symbols and logos and pictures -eg: the Eiffel tower for Paris, a red,green and white tricolour rather than the word Italian, the hammer and sickle for Russia (no longer current, but a powerful symbol that had its origins in Soviet Russia), the London Tube sign, the Mercedes star, a smiling sun, an umbrella, a tank, a laptop screen, arrows, $, £, €, etc.

Use highlighters. Have some fun - and remember, a picture is worth a thousand words - ESPECIALLY when used for presentation notes. These sorts of notes are not only easier to create, they are MUCH faster to create, infinitely easier to use and work WITH the brain rather than against it.

SECRET NO.13

GET NOTICED BY YOUR PEERS AND THOSE WHO MATTER - RAISE YOUR PROFILE NOT YOUR EGO

Being able to present well, coherently and engagingly is more than ever a prerequisite for promotion. If you can't present well, you are likely to be passed over or sidelined. Tough but true.

One of the most powerful means to do this is to present and engage confidently and eloquently. If necessary, to do so at the drop of a hat. It allows your natural talents and personality to shine through and be noticed, without having to boast, blag, brag or play politics.

Unless you choose to!

Think of those speakers you've seen and heard who've exuded that sense of confidence and calm and being in control. It's hard sometimes not to feel envious at their way of being. And we have all witnessed the sort of confidence that manifests as cocky and over weaning and self satisfied. Few things can turn an audience off faster.

If you choose to work with me, you'll build a natural sense of confidence, that comes from the inside, from an inner knowing. It isn't bolted or sprayed on from the outside - the seed is planted and watered and nurtured from within. I guarantee it.

It's been a pleasure sharing these "13 Secrets" with you. As you will by now have realised, it is a VERY small percentage of people who combine even a few of them together. I hope that you'll now be joining this select and growing band.

You'll find some useful videos on my Youtube channel ThePresentationMaestro.

If you would like a Kindle version of theses 13 Secrets, you can purchase it on Amazon today. My book, *Blow Your Own Horn* and my popular audio series *99 Tips for Successful and Powerful Presenting* are also available on my website. I have made them available here:

www.presentationskillscoaching.co.uk/products.

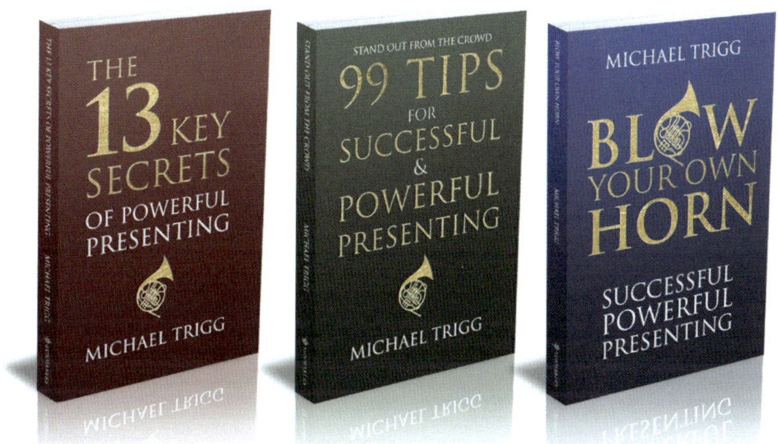

If you'd like to explore things further, without pressure or obligation, call my office on +44 208 237 5600 or mail me at greatpresenting@me.com

NOTES

NOTES

ABOUT THE AUTHOR

Michael started his working life with 5 years as a soldier before flirting with finance in a merchant bank for 2 years, where he learned that managing the money of others was not his metier.

He then joined Procter and Gamble for 6 years. Of the many valuable things they taught him, he learned that growing your people was as important as growing the business - and to reward both in equal measure.

Since helping others develop their potential was becoming a passion, he joined The Mast Organisation to pursue this full time.

In 2000 he founded Phoenix International.

He works mostly with senior management, board members, CEOs and entrepreneurs who need to engage with clients, employees and shareholders. Almost without exception they cut their preparation time by over 70%, become more interesting and engaging, more authentic and get their message across EVERY time.

He has worked with over 50 different organisations and 60 different nationalities.

Michael lives in the Cotswolds. His passions include music, the piano, theatre, the arts, food and cooking, growing vegetables, photography, Reiki, a sense of humour and almost anything that Apple creates.

WHAT PEOPLE ARE SAYING ABOUT MICHAEL

"...as a result of the fantastic work he did, he has since been referred across the organisation and the group. He has been a delight to work with... real passion and commitment and many years of experience... I have no hesitation whatsoever in recommending him. Michael cares about what he does and delivers value each and every time."

— Connie Phillips, Head of Learning and Development CMG Europe

"...I learned something new about the presentation of myself and my ideas, and it made me more effective. The second pleasant surprise is the effect the training has had on us as an organisation. We've become collectively a lot clearer in what we have to say, we've become a lot more self-confident, open and accessible... and I think part of the credit is due to Michael Trigg and his training. Thoroughly recommended."

— Dan Smith, Secretary General of International Alert

"Michael provides a framework that when used for presentations, increases their effectiveness, and thus the effectiveness of the presenter. Building on this presentation architecture, he transformed my personal presentation style using a combination of tools and experience. This combination of new presentation structure and personal style transformed my approach and dramatically improved my effectiveness."

— Mike Rushmore, Director, Markit

"I have always disliked giving presentations and wanted to know how people do this successfully without sounding like they are reading from a script. Michael gave me the tools to do this and the confidence to go on to speak in front of 150 people. His patience, understanding and obvious skills make this a painless and dare I say enjoyable process!"

— Penny Verbe, CEO of Smoke and Mirrors

"...I thought there wasn't much I could learn about Presentation Skills, but Michael proved very quickly that you certainly can teach an old dog new tricks... I finished the course thinking it was one of the best I'd ever attended in the whole of my career. As a result, I sent many of my staff to work with him. In this present economic climate, the ability to get your message across to customers both old and new is extremely important. I believe that Michael is one of the best in the industry and I can't recommend him highly enough... if you trust your training to him, you'll be delighted with the results and see the benefits in improved sales and improved skills of your staff."

— Tony Hampson, Director, MOR Facilities Management

"My session with Michael has been hugely valuable and I thoroughly recommend working with him. Michael is incredibly encouraging and knows how to get the best from people. After just one day, Michael completely changed my attitude and approach to presenting and I am now armed with excellent techniques and some new found confidence. I can't thank him enough!"

— Jenny McMahon, Account Manager, Weber Shandwick

"...Michael first worked with me 15 years ago... helped hone and develop my skills, which I use to this day. Since then, I've taken Michael to 4 different companies... introduced him to senior plc executives who've worked personally with him to develop their skills... all of it a huge success. Everybody who's worked with him has said "That's the best course I've ever been on / the best person I've ever worked with."

— Tim Hancock, Group Business Director, Connaught PLC

"...after the event I had a lot of managers approaching me... wanting Michael to come back and work with their teams and with individuals. Fantastic feedback... very professional... very thorough... I'd recommend Michael thoroughly. From a commercial point of view, you see a true value from the investment."

— Anita Way, Director, Head of Education and Development,
UBS Wealth Management

"I've just spent 2 days with Michael, and I must say it feels very good right now.

Before these 2 days, I thought the quality of my presentations was a little unpredictable.... I think I'm a FACTOR OF FIVE FOLD more influential as a result of this. If you have a similar need, I do recommend you take this course. It's REALLY REALLY VALUABLE."

— Jan Olin, MD, MobiTV Europe

"This man is excellent and I would highly recommend him."

— Chris UnderwoodHead of Communications, International Alert

"...the great thing has been that I now find that I am approaching presentations in a far more confident and relaxed manner... we've been able to secure a considerable amount of work and get our ideas across clearly to our potential customers – and this is due in no small part to the training Michael has given to us. I couldn't recommend his training too strongly."

— Allan Broad, Business Development Manager, Connaught plc

"...I've just spent 2 days with Michael 1:1... an excellent experience... I've really exceeded my expectations... feel much more comfortable in engaging with an audience... very convinced that I've made significant progress."

— Ralph Odermatt, MD, Capital Markets, UBS AG, Zurich

"Michael is a great professional and fun to work with and fun to learn from. Results guaranteed."

— Rafael Calvo, Partner, Mezzvest

"I worked with Michael about a year and a half ago. Having worked in the industry for a while and been presenting to clients for many years, I thought "How much more can I learn?" I got a bit cocky about it. But actually, the course was fantastic. It teaches you how to really structure your thoughts, to really read your audience's mind before you walk in so that you can speak and structure your thoughts around them. It teaches you clarity and the pitfalls around what to do and what not to do.

The benefits for me were realised very soon after the course. We had to go to Egypt to pitch for a job. I remember getting the brief from my boss and thinking "You can't be serious! 24 hours to turn this job round?" I was beside myself with anxiety, but I really applied the stuff I'd learned from Michael. And in 24 hours I turned it around and created a great presentation with great ideas. Went to Cairo, pitched, and a couple of weeks later we'd learned we'd got the job. And as far as I'm concerned, that wouldn't have been possible without the training course that I attended with Michael."

— Nader Khosrovani Associate Director for Strategy, Futurebrand

"I employed Michael in preparation for a major series of presentations and I have to say, I consider him to be an exemplary coach and support for all those key presentation performances in your career. Many presentation trainers seem to take all of their wisdom from books or other trainers, but Michael is 100% original: he doesn't replay knowledge from books, he shares insights that can only be acquired from a lifetime's experience. This is in itself would justify his very reasonable fees, but Michael offers much more in the way he approaches training. As well as being a very genuine person, he cares about the people he coaches and understands that there's often an internal 'confidence' dimension to coaching anyone who wishes to become a superior presenter. With Michael's help, I believe I am now on this journey."

— Jonathan Brayshaw, MD, The Original Agency Limited

"Michael is a consummate professional. What I particularly value about Michael is his ability to get the absolute best out of each individual by concentrating on their strengths. This may sound easy but it requires real skill and patience. I have also come to admire the way he prepares himself so thoroughly before each programme .The client always feels that Michael has taken the time to understand his or her business."

— Paul de Zulueta, Chief Executive, Lifestep

"I have had the pleasure of working with Michael for over seven years now, including during my time at a previous company. I first hired Michael to deliver a high profile workshop to a group of our business leaders just before a large bid presntation. Michael's innovative approach was found to be hugely engaging by the group who came away with a high impact approach that resulted shortly afterwards in two major contract wins. I have hired Michael consistently since that date and his interventions always deliver results. I have also been very fortunate to have been trained by Michael myself and I use his techniques in every presentation I give. His manner and enthusiastic style are contagious. I regularly recommend him to my clients and would have no hesitation in engaging him with any business leader."

— Mark Cooper, Director of People Development at Europa

"I've know Michael for 8 years since attending a presentation course. Michael applies a highly interactive, high energy and focused approach to training. I would recommend anyone considering presentations training to speak with Michael first, as the key skills that I learned from the presentation course delivered by Michael have been invaluable and very useful in my career to date."

—Tony Mainwaring, Operations Director, CBRE Management Services

"Before embarking on Michael's Presentation Masterclass, I had the passion to want to present and deliver a compelling presentation to different audiences but something in me at times had a mental block and this effected my confidence, amongst other things.

Through Michael's training I learnt brilliant techniques and proven methods for how to create a killer, powerful presentation! Also with Michael's coaching during the course I was able to break through the barriers related to confidence and I can honestly say that ever since I had the training, my presentation skills have increased dramatically! Thank you Michael, for you have changed my ability to present and it happened in only 2 days.

I would highly recommend anyone who is looking to gain confidence, techniques and skills in presenting to work with Michael."

— Claire Koryczan, Head of Business Development, DECODED

"What Michael taught me in two days has become a part of my thinking pattern and has helped me better think and express myself. Thanks Michael."

— Farrokh Derakhshani, Director, Aga Khan Award for Architecture

"Before working with Michael I already had extensive experience of delivering presentations, so I was delighted to find out just how much he could help me improve. As well as improving my confidence, Michael was able to show me new ways of preparing for presentations that both make the process less time consuming and improve the final result.

A few months after working with Michael I was able to test my new skills when asked to speak at a conference event. Preparation that would previously have taken me days took just a couple of hours and the presentation itself felt easier and was a great success."

— Louisa Clarke, Director of Finance, Boston Mayflower

"I owe Michael and his method of presentation training a great deal of thanks.Since attending Michael's training session I have used the presentation method repeatedly and have had the most amazing feedback! The method taught gives confidence and allows an ease with presenting without overriding your own personal style.

I wouldn't hesitate to refer Michael to any individual or firm who recognises the importance of slick, smart presentation and people skills."

— Rebecca White, Hart Brown Solicitors

"I asked Michael to 'sharpen' my presentation skills ahead of a crucial training event my company was due to run. Quite simply I was blown away by the rapid improvement that Michael achieved with me.

Michael not only improved my delivery skills but also taught me powerful techniques for reducing preparation time, structuring and sign-posting the content and how to speak completely without notes, and yet remember everything.

I was so pleased with what we achieved that I hired Michael again to work with the rest of our team.

My only regret is that I didn't learn this stuff 15 years ago."

— Andy Gooday, Brand Headhunter

TAKING YOU TO THE NEXT LEVEL

As with so many things in life - reading about something is one thing. Doing it is another. Especially when that *something* is as experiential and unique as your presenting.

As a thank you for buying and reading this book, let me give you something personal and of value.

I'd like to offer you a FREE 30 MINUTE consultation and coaching with me - worth £350.

All you have to do is complete the brief questionnaire on the webpage below and we will get back to you to schedule the call.

www.presentationskillscoaching.co.uk/nextlevel

I look forward to engaging with you and helping take you to the next level.

18657883R00033

Printed in Great Britain
by Amazon